Flowers from the Farm

Melissa Domiati

Copyright © 2024 Melissa Domiati

The rights of Melissa Domiati to be identified as the author of the work has been asserted by her in accordance with the Copyright Act of Australia, 1968.

All rights reserved.

No part of this book may be reproduced or transmitted in any form or by any means, electronic or mechanical, including photocopying, recording or by any information storage and retrieval system, without prior permission in writing from the publisher.

For any enquiries or permissions, the publisher can be contacted at melissa.domiati@thelongevitylab.com.au

First published in Australia by: Melissa Domiati

Cover Image Copyright: Jordan Fisk

First Print: 2024

ISBN [Paperback]: 978-0-6486129-1-9

For Salem
There are not enough words to describe how grateful I am that we found each other, but here are a few that I dedicate to you.

When your eyes held mine
(that very first time)
I fell for you
you smiled,
because you knew
at that moment
I knew
you loved me too.

As I held your eyes
I realised
the best of
the rest of
my life had arrived.

I would like to thank all the wonderful women in my life, in particular my daughters, Zara May and Paris Belle who have taught me so much about life and love, and still do every single day. I thank my beautiful Mum - Lyn, who always sees the light, Nanna May who taught me kindness, my first friend, Peta who remembers everything and my mother in law, Leila who welcomed me instantly into her heart.

Wondrous women, you have been the roots of inspiration, the petals of encouragement, and have cultivated the fertile soil from which Flowers from the Farm has blossomed.

Thank you to Shoma Mittra for her valuable guidance, patience and support in bringing my words into print.

I truly appreciate all the people in my life who feel like sunshine, for being the ever-present garden of my growth and creativity.

I acknowledge the traditional custodians of the lands where my poems were written. I acknowledge the cultural diversity of all Aboriginal and Torres Strait Islander peoples and pay deep respect to Elders past, present and future. My dear Nanna May, known as 'Sis' to many, had so many friends from all walks of life frequently call her front two rooms home, any time they needed a place to rest from their travels. I am grateful to call Boorlo, Perth my home, my place to rest.

Contents

Introduction	xi
PLANTING	**1**
Flowers from the Farm	3
Planting	4
Rollercoasting	5
Why I write	6
My pen	7
Your words	9
My words	10
Perfectly penned	13
Life's storytelling	14
Parchment	15
A seedling	16
Buds	18
Caffeine and friendship	19
Raw	22
Sometimes sleep	25
All is well	27
ROOTS	**29**
My roots	31
Questions for Ann Tapper	32
My Coogee Beach childhood	35
The island shack - Yunderup	44
Nanna May's recipe book	48
My child	52
The silent teen	55
School bully days	58
Hope bleeds	61
Rollover	62
Two lives	68

A very heavy coat	81
Brad's bookcase	84
She sees the light	86
Only as young as	88
Captain	89
Paperbark	92
Circles of dementia	95
Visiting hours	98

SOWING SEEDS OF ADVENTURE 101

Fly	103
A tapestry of travel	104
Gypsy girl	105
A passport	106
The wind	107
A recipe for life	108
Come fly with me	109
A wondrous world awaits	110
Meditating	111
View from a plane	113
New thoughts come from new places	114

WILTING 117

If I could	119
Buried	120
If I let you in	121
Stay	122
Fog	123
Why?	124
Broken glass	125
Close that door	126
Loneliness	127
Lost and found	128
An afterthought or a maybe	129
A song unsung	130
Sway	131
Not your table	132
Sometimes	134

Burnout	135
Pandemic mind	136
Clouds	137
Treading water	138
Rain	139
Safe in the dark	140
Storm	142
Grateful	143
Tired soles	144
Rise again	145

GROWTH 147

Woman	149
Sunday	150
Our strength	152
On course	153
Treasure within	154
Inner child	155
Little things	156
My brother told me	157
Happiness is a choice	158
Garden of friendship	161
My pool inside	165
Sleep's sublime embrace	169
A sacred space	171
To be	174

BLOOM 175

Bloom	177
The first time	178
Unlocked door	179
Our story	181
Morning	183
Love leapt in	184
The pleasure of your words	185
He reads me	186
Tightrope	187
Love is a verb	188

Immortalised in ink	189
Don't love in pencil	190
Passion	191
A giddy young girl	192
Thinking of you	193
Retreat	194
I love the way you love me	195
Whilst moonbeams trace	197
He loves me	198
As one	199
My world	201
I do	202
About the Author	203

Introduction

Anthology is a word derived from the Greek word 'anthologia', from anthos meaning 'flower' + 'logia' denoting 'collection' or to 'gather', often employed to represent a collection of 'flowers' of verse; a selection of poems or prose often comprised of work by various artists.

This collection is solely mine, inspired and supported by others but represents the very different voices I have spoken during diverse journeys in my life. I appreciate the connection with my community and reflect on my mental health struggles as well as the immense joy given to me by my two beautiful daughters Zara May & Paris Belle. There is much comfort, strength and empowerment within my words as I 'write to breathe' I give a voice to my near death experience, my struggle with losing my brother to cancer and my Mum's decline with dementia. I also write of finding my one true love.

My words have blossomed into 'Flowers from the Farm' written within the support of fellow writers, whilst we are serenaded by the train rumbling past City Farm in East Perth, nearby to where I now live with my beloved husband, Salem.

This bouquet I present to you, from deep within me. It is raw, uncomfortable, uplifting, exciting and somewhat terrifying to print

Introduction

these words for others to read. Some parts you will feel me wilting, scattering seeds, planting, growing and eventually blooming with love.

I hope in some small way you feel comforted, challenged, empowered or encouraged to express your own voice; I truly thank you for listening to mine.

Melissa Domiati
2024

PLANTING

Flowers from the Farm

Our wondrous world of words
    flourishes on the edges
    quintessential quandaries
quietly quilled
sometimes shrilled
the train shudders on its tracks
behind our backs
peeking through the sunflowers
it watches over us
rumbling its response to tales
of daylight
to darkness
writers at the farm
we plant seeds every meeting
to grow within the garden
of friendship wherein
our wonderful world of words revolve.

Planting

With our words
    we plant gardens
      or water in the weeds
fertilise the flowers
or burn down the trees.

Rollercoasting

Life.
      Glamorous, glorious
      heart wrenching and laborious
amazing, awful, ordinary
uplifting, depressing.
Life.
It always keeps us guessing
we feel unbelievably blessed
then suddenly stressed
even bored, ignored
overindulged, evolved.
Life.
It's a rollercoaster ride
a sensual slide
wherein we close our eyes
hold our breath
hide the terrors inside
rejoice and then glide.
Life.

Why I write

I write
    to fight
    the disquiet
betwixt the mind and heart of me
I converse
through verse
to breathe.

My pen

My pen
    my writerly friend
        together we play, portray
our valiant views via verse
from freely flowing
forever frolicking prose
to the pensive poems
we collectively compose.
Salvaging the strength we possess
we indulge our urge to obsess
rhyme, reason, time, seasons
surreptitiously succumb
to serene sensations
of sublime alliteration.
As silver nib meets
blank parchment
soot-black ink sometimes spills
scribbles or smudges
languidly lightening our load.

Melissa Domiati

I cradle the gentle weight
of your tortoise shell case
as we deliberate
contemplate our fate.
Where do our wondrous words
from fountains flow
originate?

Years condense into moments
    penned through poetry
    our essays of love in their purest form.

My pen
    my dear writerly friend
    together we think,
    to be ... perhaps,
    immortalised in ink.

Your words

Don't wield your words inside
 they're someone's survival guide.
 Solace is sought in sublime
secrets shared
spoken softly
sung sonorously to the skies
or pensively penned.
Your words
need to be heard
my witty, wise, wonderful friends.

My words

When I think

my words
    flow
    if I just let go
    and trust my inner voice
    they then can come freely
    like a trickling stream at first
    as if quenching a primal thirst
    until
    a waterfall cascades
    from my brain
    as the universe feeds
    my need
    for my words to be freed
    to be heard

no matter how
abstract and absurd
a river ruminates through me
floating full of words.

When I speak

my words
    sometimes
    slip
    stumble
    trip
    over each other as they fall from my mouth
    tumble
    fumble
    incoherent ramblings resembling speech
    that can't quite find their way out
    to reach meaning
    freeze
    so I just breathe
    quietly
    until the numbness leaves.

When I write

my words
    creep slowly
    like animals coming out of hiding
    peeping around corners
    until they feel safe

Melissa Domiati

    tentative steps
    one kitten's foot at a time
    soft
    at first uncertain
    warm
    they smooch up against my arm
    as if to coax me
    to stroke on their fur
    teasing, pleasing
    starting as a purr
    to be heard as a meow
    or at least written down for now.

Then they really come
    all a flourish of flamboyant fun
    playful puppies
    without fear
    my words coming near
    scampering on curious paws
    chasing their tails around in circles
    as if waiting for applause
    bounding bundles of joyful playful
    unlimited love
    warmth wisdom and whimsy
    collide merrily
    I delight in what words the moment brings
    elated in bliss
    it doesn't get much better than this.

Perfectly penned

Pain perfectly penned in poetry
    lies languidly in literature's linen
    sheets where souls speak in silence
where wordsmiths write their woes.

Life's storytelling

It's so compelling
    how life's storytelling
    is slow to disclose
it's best pieces of prose.
Initially the tale
is of loss and betrayal
as the pages keep turning
we see words of yearning
as new adventures unfold
protagonists embolden
epics eloquently penned
are worth reading until the end.

Parchment

When I write of my life
      my heart flows freely
      from my nib
my dreams and desires
are the parchment
on which I scribe.

A seedling

You come to me
     as a seedling
     seeking
a scaffold
to hold you
until you know
how to grow
upwards
roots
reaching
beneath
unsteady
not quite ready
to see
or be
who you really are
a shy smile
tilted head
toward the light

Flowers from the Farm

I delight
in being your guide
as you find your own way
to the sun
where you shine.

Buds

In the gardens
    of my soul
      I am whole
gratitude blooms
buds begin soft as whispers
in quiet rooms.

I shall nurture
    my garden
    day by day
    with heartfelt thanks
    in my own small ways.

Caffeine and friendship

Always too much time
      between coffees with you.

Amidst cafe clatter and chatter
    we sit, it starts
    shoulders sigh in relief
    words flow from our hearts
    no masks on our minds
    no filters for our thoughts
    without worry how the words will land
    we let them all out.

Melissa Domiati

The scent of coffee lingers
    fingers fumble on teaspoons
    no layers between us
    or our words
    no protection or pretence
    pure connection
    emotions come with a flood
    tumble out
    jumbled at first
    but oh how good does it feel
    to let all those thoughts
    that scream
    and cry
    and shout
    and whisper in our minds out?

Our words heard
    our feelings seen
    the taste of caffeine mingles in between
    our laughter
    we try
    looking into eyes known since childhood
    not to cry
    but that's ok too
    a hand reaches out when we do.

We understand each other's ways
    so many days of friendship
    of knowing and growing
    no walls to crumble
    nor time to waste
    knocking them down.

Flowers from the Farm

. . .

As we breathe
    our words dance free
    swirling, twirling
    safe within the confidence of you and me
    who both speak silence fluently
    we don't need answers
    our minds have them inside which will come
    when our thoughts held too tightly
    are released out of our heads
    into the gentle hands of a friend.

Months pass
    sometimes years
    we find each other again
    exactly where we are at
    when we are together
    whether a little more on track
    or further astray
    I am so grateful for the way
    our strength within
    is replenished by our friendship
    so raw, true
    always too much time
    between coffees with you.

Raw

Raw peeled back
    friends stripped bare
    are the best kind of friends
they know all your ugly bits
parts that are hidden
behind what you find
others don't want to see
scars tucked neatly
under designer clothes
they know they're there
stripped bare.

Real friends
    raw
    love you
    even more
    peeled back
    sore

from fighting battles
for good and even evil
stripped of pretence
no defence
bare it all.

Raw peeled back
    friends stripped bare
    see beyond
    cloth stained
    with the remains of pain
    washed, soaked, spun
    rags of sorrow
    sewn, stitched so deep
    needles into flesh
    weep
    tied nicely with a bow
    those parts you let show
    strip bare.

Raw peeled back
    friends stripped bare friendship
    doesn't fade
    like a holiday tan
    when confessions made
    mistakes
    don't make you
    guilt is built
    by voices in your head
    that whisper and shout
    you need to let them out
    stripped bare.

Melissa Domiati

. . .

Raw peeled back
    friends stripped bare
    know about your broken pieces
    shattered hearts
    cut by the sharpened people
    crooked cracked
    thoughts
    not shared as you are getting your hair
    cut in front of mirrors
    peeled back
    raw friends
    never judge
    when you are blunt edged
    dull
    or wedged
    between life and love and loss
    can't breathe
    off track
    filled with fears of falling
    into habits you don't want back
    stripped bare.

Your
    raw peeled back
    friends stripped bare remain
    because they see you
    between the cracks and the stains
    despite the fight, the pain
    they see your light
    raw
    love you even more.

Sometimes sleep

Sometimes sleep
      you elude me
      sometimes sleep
you tease me
make me feel I can fall easily
into you.

Sometimes
    all unease simply leaves
    as my mind finds my pillow
    thoughts billow in my sheets
    as you lift them away
    I burrow below bed covers
    you give me the balm to calm all anguish
    to follow my breath to my dreams.

Melissa Domiati

Sometimes sleep
> it seems as if you wish to play with me
> make my day stay with me
> when I wish it would leave
> I plead as I read seeking to see you
> Keats throws poppies around my bed
> yet you remain out of reach.

This time sleep
> please catch me as I fall
> heavy in your weightless embrace
> *o soft embalmer of the still night*
> allow me to delight
> in delicious drowsiness
> as your gentle oh so small lips
> close my eyes
> with kind, careful kisses
> to hush the *casket of my soul.*

All is well

All is well
      you are safe
      you are sleepy
let yourself fall deeply
you are loved
you are worthy
you are heard
take this deep rest you deserve
knowing you are held.

All is well.

ROOTS

My roots

My roots descend
    from a thousand
    loves before me.
My fledglings
fly free
a thousand lives
after I end.

Questions for Ann Tapper

A ship called the 'Rockingham'
    crashed
      on the shore
lashed
by cyclonic winds
so the records say
with my great great great grandmother
Ann
on board
baby inside
as ship and shore
collide
she met this land
this foreign sand
after miles and hours and months of waves
seeking shelter in caves
huddled
with her beloved
Daniel

and three more children
in her arms.

I wonder, was this ever your plan?

Bringing a baby
    to be born
    on the shores
    of a cumbersome
    cold
    sandy
    camp called 'Clarence'
    across tumultuous seas

What were you seeking?
    From what were you fleeing?

How did she survive?
    keeping kids alive
    the trek
    through the sand
    bush, mud, flies.
    What went through her mind?
    Fremantle
    was a long walk away
    in clothes appropriate
    for a continent
    long forgotten
    or longed for?
    I wish I could ask her.

Melissa Domiati

. . .

No register of her death
    or that of her husband
    despite it being the law
    of all the questions I had
    I now have even more.

My Coogee Beach childhood

My idyllic
       always felt like summer
       Coogee beach childhood
feels like beach sand
holding hands
walking up bitumen hills
to the lookout
jumping off the jetty
sliding down dunes
hot on our feet
next time we'll bring shoes
boys jumping off the roof
straight into the pool
welcoming cool
blister-hot days
turning the fish pond
into a spa
freedom
endless summer

Melissa Domiati

collecting shells and memories
using the pay phone to call afar
my summer job in the store
cool room bliss
filling fridges never a chore
hot cold antithesis
extremities of childhood
in all our friend's lives
seemingly no societal divide
through innocent eyes
running under the sprinklers
no home cooling
on those days
where we played
between each others houses
or on the street
burning our feet
cycling fast down hills
hands
in
the
air
no helmets
feeling fun flowing
through
our
hair
not a care
yet we felt
we might one day melt
drinking hot water from the hose.

It sometimes felt like hot fear

frozen in fright
swimming lessons
the jetty
so long
the water
so deep
terrified of the teacher
pushing us
all children lined up in a row
off the end of the jetty
waiting as if for our execution
to dive down to bring back sand or a rock
cold fear
shivering in shock

I'll show you I can swim
    please just don't push me in.

My always felt like summer childhood
    feels like darkness
    lurking in the dunes
    nudity exposed
    creeping
    peeping instability
    never fully clothed
    we just stayed away
    also like curiosity
    wondering what was waiting
    behind that fence of war
    separating
    the quarantine station
    Woodman point

a far away fascination
weapons of war
in the ammunition dump
who was creeping
behind to make us jump?
Breaking through fences
barbed wire pierced
quite fiercely
we willingly walked
wondering
when
the shells would explode
brave brothers
went first
in case the ground burst
open.

My always sounded like summer
    Coogee childhood
    sounds like waves washing
    the forever long white beach
    seagulls squawking soaring
    the dog snoring
    in front of the cricket
    wanting to be Agnetha
    in my favourite Abba Arrival t shirt
    even when the transfer faded
    then Sandy from Grease
    performing for parents
    became ignoring
    our parents
    teenage dreaming
    Madonna, Culture Club blaring

on a crackly cassette
pausing to write down the words
being reminded
to
pronounce
words
properly
by my lovely mother
calling out numbers wrapped in paper
order number 54
yelling from the house next door
homeless echoes of fear in the old power station
crunching broken glass
birthday parties
laced dolly varden cakes
sweet sounds singing Happy Birthday
or trying not to
step on the slither of a snake
my rustling pet goanna
or the Brad's croaking frog called Gorf
Christmas carol concerts at the rundown hall.

My always smelled like summer
    Coogee childhood
    smells like
    salt
    vinegar
    sprayed on jellyfish stings
    Mum's lamingtons baking
    Sunday roast dinner
    crispy potatoes
    mint sauce in the crystal jug
    Nanna's rose scented powder

Melissa Domiati

    wet dog on my lap
    tanneries in one direction
    Watsonia the other
    hot sweat
    fish and chips
    frozen coke
    dusty cobwebbed haunted orphanage
    Sunday school
    cups of milky tea with sugar
    burnt meringues
    wafting scent of sausage rolls
    salted sea spray on the boat.

My always tasted like summer
    Coogee childhood
    tastes like sandy hot water from the hose
    sneaking Cadbury chocolate for breakfast
    would never do that at home
    wet sweet first kiss
    at the lookout
    learning how to hold hands
    wandering up & down the hill to see
    which house we would find
    the best afternoon tea
    often at mine
    my mum baked
    pink jelly cakes
    rolled in coconut flakes
    chocolate eclairs
    biscuits from mills and wares
    served on silver trays
    white lace doilies
    flowers in a vase

sweetness of summer
mixed lollies
musk sticks
icy poles on two sticks
eating ice cream with my dog in the pool
mostly on her face
milky white
on her black shiny nose.

My always looked like summer
   Coogee childhood
looks like
bush and beach and a blistering hot sky
crawling through
sprawling
claustrophobic
caves
waves
where the water nearly trapped us
where the cafes are now
exploring the quarries
before the fancy houses came
lots of dogs walking between the wooden houses
Jesus cards psalms printed
coveted awards
for colouring in between the lines
chicken pox spots on my belly
still have the cards
up the hill to friends' houses
sliding back down
on a rusty piece of tin
still have the scars
sand dunes

Melissa Domiati

caravan park
freedom to wander
peeking over the neighbour's fence
watching them water in the nude
until the cubbyhouse got moved
bumpy beat of the boat bouncing
Dad at the helm
to Garden island
broken battered cars in the quarries
before the fancy houses came
wandering back home
when the sun went down
before the street lights turn on.

Looking back through an adults lens
    we lived happily
    between
    beach
    no money for the bus
    bush
    and the start of the fancy houses
    with love
    family
    and
    friends.

Flowers from the Farm

My Coogee childhood
   always
   felt
   smelt
   tasted
   sounded
   looked
   like a hot endless summer
   so much sizzled underneath
   but we never did quite melt.

The island shack - Yunderup

A day long dusty drive
    flies and dry heat escaping
    when we wound the window down.
The searing smoke scented summer
burned against my outstretched arm
pushing out parched air
gliding
riding
the wave
like a rollercoaster
in the back seat of the car
dog - wet tongue flapping.

The barge to the island waited for us
    adult arms laden with eskies
    and precarious piles of pillows and people
    pulling the rope
    one

hand
at
a
time
moving our makeshift platform
rusty ten gallon drums
a seesaw of sorts
a balancing act with no audience
only magpies' eyes
and the fish far beneath us.

Mum's hand never letting go.

Shade welcomed us
    cooled our backs
    as did the canopy of trees protecting our shack
    dusty cobwebs holding the tin roof to the asbestos walls
    half removed posters
    remnants of tape curled up at the edges
    worn floral lino
    half hiding the floorboards that
    creaked
    in
    the
    night
    metal bunk beds
    musty smells of second hand sheets
    once-loved bedspreads tucked in tight.

Cricket's chirp in the morning
    answering the magpie's call

Melissa Domiati

    to go to the river to collect paperbark
    to write childish poetry upon
    shining sap bleeding from the trees.

Cousins, many.
    Laughter.
    First friendships.
    Black mud
    made a murky river playground
    coating ourselves in jet black sludge
    boys and girls alike
    believing we all looked the same
    Suzie - identical somehow to Mike.
    Power boats hummed
    the odour of petrol
    wafting as civilisation encroached
    on our idyllic neighbourhood
    zooming to Tatum's for fuel, bread
    or musk sticks if you had been good.

We were not expecting visitors to our shack.
    It was far away
    and took most of a full day
    to get there.

Yet, this one blistering day
    my father's brothers came.

Of eight, at least four arrived that day.
    Solemn steps on dusty ground.

Flowers from the Farm

My heart crept into my throat
wondering why they were here

I saw only shoes and sobbing
    maybe because I was small
    the first time I heard my father cry
    Poppy Les with his thick solid dairy farmer's arms
    and hands of solid steel
    was gone
    his soft heart had stopped
    in his gentle, firm embrace
    I wouldn't ever sit again.

I sat in the silent shade
    peeling back layers of soft paper bark
    coolamons of white beige grey
    no words to write that day.

(*Coolamons - traditional Aboriginal vessels related to the journey of life, new babies were wrapped in them made of paperbark as it was so soft, so my grandmother told me as I used the paper to write upon*).

Nanna May's recipe book

Country Women's Association
     I can taste the flavours of gratitude inside.
     It watches over everything.
Was it her mother's?
Her Aunt who adopted her?
I wished I asked more when she was alive
I see her beautiful smile that felt like a hug
now I seek answers in her cookbook
ingredients of memories
oh the stories it could tell.

I open the pages to a flood of love
    images come fast
    scones
    white dustings of flour
    warm moist in the centre
    like the constancy of love.
    growing up without a father

at the kitchen table
was never spoken of
as card games were played
on floral tablecloths embroidered
within Shirley's silent world where she observed it all.

Milky white tea from an bottomless pot
    kept tea cosy warm
    kettle always hot
    pink and white teacups
    faded floral Royal Doulton used every day
    they must have got them at their wedding
    but not put away for best
    gilt edged no more
    verandahs filled with travellers needing rest
    always a sanctuary for a myriad of guests
    wandering walkabout on their way
    everyone loved Nanna May
    welcomed to share in an eternal card game
    or the lolly jar with its bright red lid
    remnants of the ones the kids
    didn't like clinging to the bottom
    but always refilled
    and always lots of cousins.

Pop's sherry
    Brad used to take sneaky sips of as a boy
    smelt so sweet, I never liked it.
    scrambled eggs
    with a bit too much milk
    cooked on the metters wood stove
    dumplings plonked upon her stews

the taste of coins in the Christmas custard
given out under the clothesline out the back
the train rumbled comfortingly
on its tracks
while we showed off our new shoes
or merit certificates from assembly at school
where on Fridays
Pop drove his car slower than we walked.

I turn brittle pages and feel
    hugs into warm soft breasts
    big marshmallow pillows
    comfort
    white perfect hair
    my memory recalls the scent of lavender and rose
    tick tock tick.
    The cuckoo clock watched the kids
    I now wonder where it is?
    Colourful crochet covered the old couch
    a few stitches loose
    Pop watches the square wooden tv
    not even sure if it's turned on
    smell of cigarettes and the Pekingese dog,
    Benji. Never barked, but grumbled
    A spinning ashtray we weren't really supposed to touch
    sleepovers in the spare room with Susan
    reading the pile of Mills & Boons
    the drama they wrote we thought too much.

Flowers from the Farm

The cookbook is faded and torn
    smudged with love and worn
    with remnants of past meals and memories
    burnt even in parts
    Recipes handwritten on margins
    straight from her heart
    spills and stains
    after more than forty years
    sweet subtle scent of golden syrup remains
    I wonder of the last time she used this book
    when she hand wrote
    added notes
    'Mock snapper' - food made from whatever you had
    It wasn't really a recipe
    more of an expression of the flavours of gratitude and love.

My child

You
know
me
like no one else.
Only you have felt
my heart beat
from the inside.

Cocooned
    in my womb
    the beats of
    my heart
    serenaded
    you
    to
    strength
    those magical months
    you swayed inside of me

your heart
held beating
within my depths.

The heart beat
   you listened to
   from the inside
   became the soundtrack
   of our lives
   our knowing hearts
   beat
   in unison.

Did you know that you are all my wishes come true?
   Oh how I dreamt of you
   with your tiny hands
   I wonder
   if you will ever understand
   the waiting
   anticipating
   this unique, infinite love
   of becoming your mother
   being known by another
   who resides
   inside
   this need
   to feed
   sow, grow
   the seed of a soul
   so perfect as you.
   My cherished child
   did you know how much I wanted you?

Melissa Domiati

. . .

With your knowing heart
    please hear
    the depth of my love
    always for you
    The one that has heard my heart beating from the inside.

The silent teen

Teens
    can be
        oh so very mean
but they don't mean to be
they pull back
then attack
then don't talk to you
listen to their silence
it's filled with the noises they are trying to
decipher
to work out
where they fit
sit in their silence
it sometimes comes out
in a shout
love lurches
in loud lashings not really meant for you
don't take in the hurtful
words

Melissa Domiati

    they throw
    like arrows
    games they play
    or the way
    they ignore
    which often hurts more
    rejection
    of your affection
    is the norm
    you don't want to accept.

Deep down
    they know you are there
    you are their safety net
    to catch what's left
    after
    hormones hurt
    friends and
    the school days end
    the world
    has rejected them
    doors might slam in your face
    still
    keep yours wide open
    despite the pain
    one day they will open it back
    a crack
    a glimmer
    of the love that shone from their eyes
    when they looked up for you to teach them how to toddle
    walk
    talk
    will return

you will slowly learn
to speak their silence more fluently.

Listen
    not to respond
    but to understand
    try to not take this version
    of this temporary person
    too personally
    again you will hold their hand
    just
    not
    quite
    yet.

Listen in silence
    whilst living this continual test
    of where the boundary of your love lies
    show them
    it
    is
    endless.

School bully days

Fremantle
    train station
    lolly shop
on the way to high school
pockets full
bulging
with sweet sherbies
fun
to become
stuck in my teeth
in typing class
to share
with new friends
I'll find there.

Not used to wearing a tie
    or uniform
    but happy it provides

Flowers from the Farm

something to hide
behind
ugly
green and black polyester
stripes that strangled me
were better than going back
to where
the risk of attack
was looming
heart beat booming
in my chest
like a shout
so loud with the thought
best to
stay away
from those school days
the constant threat
dread rose in my throat
where that girl
would push me
up against the demountable
wall
punch me hard in the face
holding my neck in place
with her other hand
eyes bulging
like an evil blowfish
floating her threats
in the goldfish bowl
gloating
of being the roughest
toughest kid in the pond.

. . .

Melissa Domiati

Painful in my shyness
    tried not to be clever
    changed my answers
    so my scores
    would never
    be the best
    of the rest of the class
    trying to avoid wearing
    the label of clever
    to keep from ever
    being noticed.

New school
    was laughter with Peta
    in kind safety of my dear friend since childhood
    I found new ones
    sunbaking our legs
    outside religion class
    Linda applied eye-liner
    under the desk
    always curious as to what lollies
    I had in my pocket
    but more so in what she could find
    inside my mind.

Hope bleeds

Hope bleeds out of me
    every month
    as I cross off the days on the calendar
long days passed that I hoped I would have been your mum
loud laughter of other people's children
warms me
simultaneously scalds the cold front I wear
shards leave a hole
so inexorably hard
this piercing pain of longing
an always ache to meet you
a hope each month
a very long six years.

Rollover

Drizzling outside
    a party that day
    dark clouds in parts
of my heart
had to be pushed away.

Seeking sunshine for my kids
    not their fault
    I was not feeling well.
    Looking forward to seeing Nel
    my dear friend
    a party
    two little girls
    excited to attend.

Constructed costumes
    a pirate theme

the hours it seemed
well spent
swashbuckling swords
of cardboard
wrapped in alfoil
ready for adventure
glitter
everywhere they went.

Hands laden night-time routines
    baked to replace
    loneliness
    a recipe for love.

Hurried
    mirror makeup check
    hoping to conceal more
    than dark circles
    of the unrecognisable eyes
    who looked back at mine
    if only they were as bright
    as the light
    that sparkled in two little fair faces
    and their glittering attire.

Giggles
    clambered
    climbed into the car
    then strapped them tightly
    safely in the back
    two gentle kisses

placed
on two precious foreheads
a ritual of my own.

Presents piled precariously
    on the front seat
    wrapped in pirate paper.
    Patsy Biscoe sang
    "puff the magic dragon" confidently
    car careering on autopilot
    driving down Frenchman Bay
    winding absentmindedly into town.

Racing mind
    too much to do
    never enough time.

That corner came too quickly
    I drove this stretch
    every
    single
    day
    I should have known better
    should have slowed down
    should have stayed home.

Left tyre touches the crunchy orange gravel
    slipping
    sliding
    slow motion - too far to one side.

Flowers from the Farm

. . .

As if waking from a dream
    with a start
    it seemed
    like a slap on my face
    but in my heart
    eyes wide
    scanning
    towards the side
    of the slide
    reflex
    yanking the wheel
    overcorrect
    no time to feel
    the panic inside.

Onwards from here
    a hazy blur
    I don't think I could steer
    us back onto course
    even in
    slow
    motion
    car rolled
    all
    by
    itself
    on all angles - the three of us inside
    like clothes in a washing machine
    we tumbled
    glass smashing
    jarring

Melissa Domiati

    jolting
    suddenly
    faster now than my horse bolting
    glass, ground and gravel
    speared us from all sides
    suspended in distorted time
    until the thud
    like gunshot
    reverberating my being
    we landed
    somehow on all fours.

Halted in our tracks by a tree
    I had no air inside me.

Silence.

I looked ahead
    for what seemed
    to
    be
    hours
wondering if we were alive or dead.

I looked ahead.
    The road carpeted in colourful costumes
    littered with glistening glittering gifts
    wrapped in shattered glass and cakes
    cakes uneaten, loneliness remained
    the flavour of blood in my mouth

fear paralysed my heart beat
shoulder pierced by pain.

Trapped inside
    this jagged cage of glass and metal
    too much trepidation to turn around
    I stared ahead, instead.

Bile climbed up my throat
    together with the taste of terror
    where the air should have been.

The music had stopped within
    then the sirens squealed outside
    gasping in grief
    I turned around
    and found
    two little fair faces eyes wide
    I began to breathe the air of relief.

Two lives

I suppose I've had two lives
    maybe even more
    yet, now I think of times
after I died
rather than (my life) before.

The last day of
    (that life before)
    began like others
    packing lunches
    giggling, chores
    wiping faces
    tying shoelaces
    ironing uniforms.

Flowers from the Farm

Car filled with chatter
    and the scent of
    melting moments
    just baked
    warm dustings of icing sugar
    melted butter on paper doilies.

Anticipation
    running races
    excited faces
    routine of kisses
    on warm cheeks
    sorry to miss your race
    run fast
    good luck
    I love you!
    See you soon.

Operation
    hesitation
    routine procedure
    apprehension
    removing wisdom
    teeth I don't need
    wisdom handy sometimes
    I hoped they wouldn't take all of mine.

Wheeled in
    by Carol smiling
    with her sunflower cap
    on a trolley like at the shops

Melissa Domiati

    yet flatter
    swerving swaying
    stainless steel shining
    pushing fear from my mind
    gown gaping at the back
    hoping
    no one can see my behind.

Sterile smells
    crept up my nose
    down into my throat
    white walls
    a ticking clock
    tubes
    blur
    slur of words
    metal implements
    cold sensation
    woozy dizzy
    boozy giddy
    falling
    gone.

That way that only drugs
    can
    pull
    you
    down.

Flowers from the Farm

You are not to wake up.
    Not to pick up the girls from their carnival.
    Not to drink tea.
    Not to share the biscuits on the bench.

Oblivious
    to the flurry
    hurry
    of panicked doctors and nurses
    whirling dervishly around
    my half dead body
    my vital signs
    faded
    I curled into a hard knot
    foetal
    mortis
    heat
    muscles melted to fluid
    then rigid
    only bone left.

Malignant - deathly
    Hyperthermia - overheating
    two words
    you would never have heard
    if you didn't react
    giving me the chance to take you away.

It's too late to turn back
    it's the thing you signed
    before you went under.

Melissa Domiati

. . .

You thought it wouldn't happen to you.

Police cars screamed
    driving from towns
    all around
    a car chase
    a race
    against the clock
    to bring *Dantrolene* -
    a word I'd never seen
    before
    my antidote
    my saviour
    if administered in time.

Angels appeared
    in the form of the flying doctor
    helicopter
    they flew my body
    alone
    wrapped like leftover lunch
    in foil to keep me cool
    mind unaware
    if the kids had finished school
    for the day
    I was flown away above the clouds
    missing all the races
    no rush for parking spaces
    landing on a hospital rooftop.

Flowers from the Farm

Darkness
    pervaded my system
    inwards
    I shrank
    I felt
    low
    flat
    heavy.

Sunken to the floor and below
    antithesis of light and weight
    I was pulled
    wrenched
    called
    cajoled
    to Death.

Come to me now
    this is my command
    not a request
    your presence is demanded.

Held hostage
    in this tunnel
    of hazy hues
    a vacuum cleaner hose
    a funnel
    wide
    narrow
    writhing like a serpent
    with piercing yellow eyes

spirals of thin lights
distance crawling
closer sprawling
pulling
willing

You must come to me
　It is your time.

Gentle
　easy
　oh so pleasing
　to just blend back
　to relax
　into the pulling
　like a tidal rip
　of seduction
　suction.

Oh just take me!

Slipping
　tripping
　simpler to submit.

Melting
　just moments away
　from oblivion
　too tired to stay

    the lure of lightness
    lifting me
    swiftly
    to ultimate rest.

On my left he sat
    as if on a chair
    but with legs crossed
    how he sat before
    Cancer took him.
    His words were calm
    clear without fear
    as if through a microphone
    thin yellow fingers on my arm.

You must not come
    It is not your time

little sister
    you cannot follow me

Brad spoke in a whisper
    the pull towards him
    was magnetic
    that lifetime-long year since he left
    a family bereft
    his love
    flooding me from above
    I wanted to follow
    him to quench the hollow

insatiable thirst
the pull towards never
never coming back.

Death demanded again
   I chose not to answer.

Suddenly
   I remembered
   life
   I was strong enough to fight.

As if waking from a dream
   pierced by a fierce
   determination to stay
   with a lion's roar
   I called to my daughters
   eyes teeming with tears
   voice screaming with fear
   I turned towards darkness
   climbed
   crawled
   fought
   the long journey out.

I awoke from sleeping
   to beeping
   light
   white
   days had passed

my mouth forced open by a tube
that was breathing for me
I could not speak
even with my hands
nurses ran to me
peering wide eyed
concerned
calming
cautious
don't let my parents see me like this
they can't lose their last child
I thought I was losing my mind
I tried to sign
I can't even use
the language of the deaf
I thought
distraught
my arms didn't work
I tried with all my might
no muscles on my bones
a skeleton
a scary sight.

My daughter's fair faces
    filled with fear
    widest eyes
    searching in sunken spaces
    looking for traces
    of their mother
    missing me
    too scared to kiss me
    too short to climb up the hospital bed
    them trying to be brave

Melissa Domiati

as if next to my grave
breaking pieces of my heart with each word.

Other people washing me
    fed by a tube
    the man in the next bed
    died one night
    they closed the curtain
    wheeled him away
    on a trolley
    like in the shops.

Somedays
    I didn't want to learn to walk
    I already did that as a child
    it was too hard
    I felt sorry for me
    wanted just to scream
    to cry
    to hide
    wheelchair walks outside
    would terrify me
    going out those safety doors
    into a world where smokers huddle
    throw rubbish on the floor
    I wanted to curl back up
    in the sanctity of sterile
    where people were kind
    and I was a novelty
    to have survived.

. . .

Hours turned to
    lonely days to
    weeks to
    a year
    before I learnt to
    properly walk again
    the pain
    of growing one muscle at a time
    tear
    repair
    and tear again to grow
    so slowly
    was a new routine
    for me
    that seemed
    to be
    mine alone.

I now stand strong
    long love filled life ahead
    many years have passed
    (this life after I died)
    is a blessed one
    my girls are grown
    adults of their own
    who cared for me
    when I couldn't care for them.

Melissa Domiati

I'm grateful I'm alive
    I now cherish the time
    (in this new life)
    after I survived
    maybe more
    than I ever did before.

A very heavy coat

I often think about him.
Who am I kidding? Rarely a day goes by that he doesn't touch my world in some small way or another. A flicker of light catches my eye, my breath quickens and my heart warms with the thought of him. Then, the harsh realisation that I can't just pop in for a chat, cuts like a shard of ice.

What is he thinking now? Oh how I miss our philosophical discussions. Borrowing his 70's denim jacket. The one with the very flared collar that matched the jeans that were just that bit too big. I wonder what whimsical delight he is inventing now.

What brings him light? What would he think of my life since we were last breathing the same air? What words of wisdom would he weave for me to wonder?

I know that he still loves me, some things are permanent. Enduring. The way his face would light up the instant he saw me was all the truth that I needed to know. The way he introduced me to his myriad of friends, as an extension of him. His unwavering interest in my life, in my comings and goings. Nothing was ever too much trouble. I remember the Christmas that he drove four hours each way to be with me, just because he couldn't bear the thought of my melancholy, as he knew the celebration was important to me.

Mum told me that all he wanted as a gift for the Christmas of 1970 was an umbrella and a baby sister.

He was always so very proud of me. Despite him actually being blessed with sublime and superior intelligence, he always stood in awe every time I received an award. A degree. Some accolade or piece of paper that I attained just through the process that was required to obtain some semblance of credibility or distinction. Attained to hide the pain of not being enough.

Even without all this, he always thought I was enough. He witnessed my glow, even when I couldn't see it. He kept me warm. He gave me all his hand-me-downs. Clothes that were unflattering in many ways, unbecoming for a young lady, but warm and protecting. I still have a jacket somewhere. I also have a t-shirt from when we went to see Dylan Moran at the concert hall together, that I cannot bear to throw out. His laughter still rings in my ears. Sometimes I forget his voice, I panic, then it returns.

He still fills my dreams. Sometimes he is just sitting alongside me at the riverside. A very slow walk in the sunshine. The two of us perched on the grass, both nervously plucking out the pieces by their roots from the soil.

The day we had 'that' conversation.

The day that he told me and I really did not want to listen. Denial.

He asked me to be strong. Strong is all I am. All I had to be from that day onward.

I was desperate to fix the unfixable. I was good at solving problems, helping others, and making everything ok. This time I was failing. Failure was never an option for me. It was beyond my power to make everything ok. Slowly, as hope faded, the conversations were filled with resignation. The light was fading.

He was slowly drifting away from me. I tried to hold on, but he had other places he had to go. Places that he did not want me to come with him.

I even tried for a moment to place him on the periphery of my life. I went south. Ran away, but soon returned. That was not a long moment.

All the very long moments occurred later. They still do.

Days of long moments.

Days where Mum tried to hold everyone together. Days, when she told me many times that all Brad wanted as a gift for the Christmas of 1970 was an umbrella and a baby sister.

I think it is the tinge of yellow on his skin that burns in my memory, the gradual way his muscular body melted to bones, barely moving, placed upon a bed. A brown bottle of morphine by his bedside. The way his eyes lit up as if to say "you are here now", even when he was unable to speak.

The light appeared, then faded away in those desperate, sunken eyes of my brother, my forever friend.

Grief is love wearing a very heavy coat.

Brad's bookcase

I search solemn shelves
    hollow, sorrow pulls deep
        I ruminated in rows reserved for memories of your pain
I felt I needed to keep
tortuous truths catalogued
in the library of my heart
stories of sorrow
now need to be returned
as I touch tasselled bookmarks
placed in perfumed pages
I shall solely seek sunshine
in your volumes of valour
recorded to remember
too important to forget.

Flowers from the Farm

The hardest page to turn
   is the knowing
   you won't be in the next chapter
   yet my story must continue
   without you.

I promise you it will be an adventure story worth reading.

She sees the light

She sees light. Her kindness and positive attitude, inherited from her mother, continually inspires me to seek beauty and lightness every day and appreciate the goodness that is present in my daily life. Even when shadows loom.

We walk together, Mum and I together in the sunshine alongside the inlet. She smiles and waves at small children running past or sitting up in their strollers. Gives gentle words of encouragement to their parents, about how lovely their shoes are or the way the light bounces off their curly hair. She giggles freely with elderly ladies ambling along absentmindedly with their carers. She chats equally to dogs and their owners, remarking on the exuberance that being free in the sunshine encourages.

Whilst Mum interacts with the world, I hold her elegant, slender hand and watch in silence. I marvel at her easy grace and gentle way of kindness and connection. She makes people smile. Makes people feel seen. She shines bathed in her own serene light. She speaks words of positivity that may well have been the only human interaction those people experience on those days. I am so lucky that I am able to feel the warmth of my Mum's light every day when I talk to her.

This image might sound unremarkable, but it stops me in my tracks. Enough to pen this note to share and mark this day. How often do we allow ourselves to pause and be astonished by those who surround us? How often do we look up when we are walking and smile at people, noticing their differences and the beauty they exude? Do we ever notice the way the light hits peoples hair and bounces off it, or their eyes reflect the sunlight so generously? Most often we don't.

My Mum does.

She might be forgetting some things lately, but she doesn't forget to notice and be amazed at what begs to be marvelled at. She remembers to notice the sparkles of light that exist when people connect, even for a fleeting moment before she retreats back within. That mischievous smile sneaks out of the corner of her mouth when she says ' Oh, I am cheeky, just like my Mother. I talk to everyone. They don't mind. They need to know that they are seen and are special.'

Whenever something goes well, or I notice the good in a situation I think of how Mum, despite her own light fading with Alzheimer's disease finds a way to notice the light in little things. I hope that this little piece of light from my beautiful Mum might just reach you if you need to hear it.

Only as young as

She is only as old as the number of times
    she's seen the sun rise and set
    spirits soothed her soul
she's heard champagne pop
smelt caffeine's bliss
explored new places
tried something new
hugged her loved ones with pride
felt her babies kick.

She's only as young as the number of times
    her heart skipped a beat
    love sparkled in her eyes
    breathless from laughter
    she felt a forehead kiss.

Captain

I see you
     steering one handed
     drifting off course
grip softening with time
the tide of understanding
travelling in and out
challenges crashing daily
rocking, rolling off course
pushing against a current
wading in the worries
of the one you love most.

Melissa Domiati

I hear you
    now wholly in charge
    of holding the memories afloat
    watching waves crash
    once you were cared for
    now the carer
    facing fears so foreign
    fighting the flow of time
    pulled away in a rip
    too treacherous to admit.

I see her
    seeking safe anchorage
    in the harbour of
    holding your hand
    her childhood sweetheart
    security and solace
    always alongside her
    her constant companion
    the one she adores
    more than herself.

I feel you
    struggling
    resisting rescue
    giddy on the shore
    stepping on shifting sands
    of isolation
    withdrawing from the world
    the sea sonorously singing
    songs of love
    your life gently swaying

Flowers from the Farm

feel the warmth of the sand
the earth holds you both
the love you give gently
comes back to you
with the ocean's breath
the sigh of the tide
in her smile
reminding
she is always with you.

Paperbark

Loneliness
      is hollow
       a shallow sound
that echoes inside me
as I sit empty
breaking, aching
in the shade of her fragility.

She fades before my eyes
    paperbark falls to the floor
    floating fragments of frailty
    branches break one by one
    her journey back to earth has begun.

Flowers from the Farm

It's the slowest agony
    of privilege
    to hold her hand
    now she no longer understands
    thin, soft papery skin
    like the bark
    we peeled from the trees together
    to write stories on
    smooth, soft silvery sheets
    are her fingers that squeeze mine
    strong, gentle, fine
    she sits with me
    while her mind slowly leaves
    to other places
    traces
    of her stories remain
    whispered in the wind through the leaves.

It's the fading that breaks me
    she would never forsake me
    by choice
    but now
    from one who always bloomed
    no new buds are growing
    and I must be her voice.

Melissa Domiati

Her eyes reach out to the distance
    as if she cannot see me
    amongst the trees
    yet she is grounded
    roots so deep
    surrounded
    by her ancestors
    as she slips in slow
    slumbering steps one by one
    her passage back to country has begun.

Circles of dementia

So much I want to ask you
    yet the
        whirling words
in my mind won't stay long enough
to let me
I fret, as fragments sneak out in circles
around what I want to say
words won't flow
they go
round and round
up and down
like your favourite
merry-go-round at the zoo
my words are all in circles
yet, they always come back to you.

Melissa Domiati

I want you to know I see you
    your kindness
    encircles others as you shine
    despite
    my light fading with each moon
    your bright sun's glow
    makes me smile
    all the while
    sentences skip around
    inside my mind.

I find, you
    see-sawing in the playground
    up and down
    balancing other people
    as they play
    now time has come full circle
    to let them find their way.

I want to show you
    how to make time
    stop spinning around
    you go too fast
    on that dizzy wizzy ride
    the slippery slide
    is steep
    I want to guide you
    away from rush and flurry
    always in a hurry
    my words go round in circles
    yet what I'm trying to tell you
    is put those lists away

it doesn't all have to be done today.

I want you to know I'll always be here
    even when my body has gone
    this long goodbye is slow
    but I won't ever truly go
    in the melodies of my mind
    a music box dancer forever twirls
    for my little girl
    you can see me in the moon
    I will peek through the window
    bathe you in my light
    day and especially at night
    while you sleep
    I will watch over you
    like the child you were
    always will be
    to me.

My circles, like the moon
    will always come back to you.

Visiting hours

It is not far away
    until the day
        that I will have to wait until
visiting hours
to see you.

As a child
    I could call you
    you would come to my bedside
    tuck me in
    warm within
    freshly ironed bed sheets
    wrapping me up safely
    arms firmly by my side
    you would turn off the light
    kiss my forehead
    and all my thoughts goodnight.
                . . .

Flowers from the Farm

I could walk up each stair
    in the morning
    towards the smell of toast
    running late for school
    or uni
    or work
    to find you in the kitchen
    surrounded by the aroma of
    comfort and coffee
    your smile
    your love
    neatly packaged into a lunch box
    to take with me wherever I needed to go.

I could drive the highways from wherever I roamed
    back to you as was my whim
    to give you a hug
    whenever I wanted to
    but soon
    too soon
    it will be only
    around constructed
    visiting hours that I will be able to see you.

I could no longer
    your love is not restricted to visiting hours,
    but I know the time is coming
    too soon
    slowly you will forget who I am
    but I remember you.
    No visiting hours for your love
    always open.

Melissa Domiati

. . .

A chair is missing
    where you used to sit
    at the dinner table
    it is easier to look at
    the space
    than an empty chair.

SOWING SEEDS OF ADVENTURE

Fly

Time
　　flies past
　　　so very fast
you are the pilot
fly.

A tapestry of travel

My life is a journey
      without a map
      a tapestry of travel
seamlessly stitched
with song lyrics
the scent of coffee
breathing in salt air
whilst glasses clink.
Interwoven moments
with souls who fill my heart
in undiscovered places
this exquisite fabric of life
is an adventure of exploring
the smiles I'd like to keep.

Gypsy girl

Gypsy girl
     eyes wide with wanderlust
     desire for discovery
dances in her wings
whilst adventure fills
her solivagant's soul.
She travels
not to find herself
but to remember
who she always has been.

A passport

A passport
 is a storybook of our lives
  let's take off into
this wondrous world
and fill its pages together.

The wind

Inhale her breath
    be enveloped in the essence
    of her most exquisite embrace
feel her flurry, her flutter
whirling dervishly inside you
she's a rising storm
here to clear your path.

She shall hold you forever
    embedded with the love
    of the souls that protect you
    with the wind whisper in your wings
    you shall be shown the way
    she shall never leave you lonely
    always trust in the wind.

A recipe for life

Inhale read
    exhale write
    breathe
repeat.

Come fly with me

Come fly with me
      let's fly
        let's fly away
we'll make wings
from broken things
and soar across the skies.

A wondrous world awaits

She sleeps
    her heart held
        in the softness of slumber
amidst Morpheous' musings
love lingers longingly
she wakes
a wondrous world awaits.

Meditating

I'm currently
    recalibrating
    waiting
for the cogs to realign
in my mind
I'm gently
anticipating
space
to
embrace
the quiet.

Melissa Domiati

Sometimes
    I find
    in my mind
    there are
    too
    many
    tabs
    open.

Some need to close
    so I can let go
    of thoughts
    that
    float
    in
    give them permission to leave.
    When I am still
    they will.

Often
    I find
    when I am kind
    to myself
    I let go of fear.

The quieter I am
    the more I can hear.

View from a plane

After take off
    what holds me down
    falls away
gets left behind
with the miniature buildings
little boxes that
confine my mind
shrink
disappear
fade as I squint
I then let go
of little thoughts
large views
inspire large thoughts
what I see
what I am able to think about
widens with the clouds.

New thoughts come from new places

I wonder
    how this cumbersome bird
    holding me
in the sky
always opens my mind.
Curiosity
my constant companion
(travelling on a plane)
growth happens
with each adventure
we cannot return the same.

Maybe it's the movement
    (same happens on a train)
    views distracting us from
    normality
    and all that is mundane
    banality

of being bored
of the everyday
routines of familiar feelings
impedes creativity
if you focus on difficulties
or the dishes.

With a moving view
    separate from you
    can't shy away from desires
    feelings, longings
    memories that arise
    on voyages
    views villages flashing past
    so fast
    too much so
    to know
    where the people are going
    more open to ideas
    mind uncluttered by fears
    watching the train carriage door
    how it closes
    or the tray table of an airline seat
    knees knocking against tray tables.

Harsh lighting
    keeps us writing
    dull decor demands we feel alive.
    In an airport lounge we thrive
    isolation
    of a train station
    stark

Melissa Domiati

harsh in its contrast
to the
ease of home habits
structure and
confines of the ordinariness
left behind
our creativity we find.

WILTING

If I could

If I could
    I would
        ask for
just one more day
with you.

But if I could
    have that one day
    I would see
    that one more day
    could never be enough
    for me.

I want more time with you.

Buried

Buried
      beneath a blanket of bewilderment
      banished
betwixt bereavement
and the banality of being
bereft.

If I let you in

My heart
    my soul
      my life
I may let you in
if I do
please don't break anything.

Stay

Breathe, don't leave
      don't burrow away
     stay
curl close to me
I speak silence
fluently.

Fog

Though fog pervades your brain
    you'll find the fortitude to glimpse again
    that infinitesimal luminous sight
filtering through ever so slight
so you can see to climb
one small step at a time
despite the dark
you'll discern the light
it's not in your blood to lose this fight.

Why?

Why do emotions
      sneek
        creep
climb
from the deep
into your throat
choke
then glide
slide
so surreptitiously
out of your eyes?

Broken glass

Don't try to break off a piece
    of my robust, ruby heart
        my magnificent mosaic of mirrors
has before been broken apart
perfect pieces previously pasted
into precise positions unmarred
once shattered
battered, broken
are now sheltered from the shards
a kaleidoscope of strength reflects
my rediscovered soul
putting back my inner self
has truly made me whole.

As beautiful as broken glass may shine
    be gentle if you covet mine.

Close that door

You are no carpet to be wiped on
      or revolving door
        to be walked through
again and again.

That's enough now!
    Remove the carpet
    close that door
    it's time to walk away.

Loneliness

Loneliness gnaws at her
      biting, tearing at her flesh
      chewing on her heart
spitting out the pieces
too painful to digest.

Lost and found

I came upon a box
    with 'lost & found' inscribed
    I found you within it
then lost myself inside.

Now that I've since lost you
    I found myself again
    I'll no longer fit into boxes
    where no room for me remains.

An afterthought or a maybe

You left me raw
    skin peeled back
    bare heart in view.

I am not here for you
    to enjoy the ride
    to be cast aside
    I am worth so much more
    than an afterthought
    or a maybe.

A song unsung

The hum of faraway tunes
    is not enough
    aching
absent minded touch
pain
pangs like an afterthought
if my song is not heard
I'd rather not sing along
to melancholy tunes
my song unsung
waits silently
unheard.

Sway

Sing with me
    sway
    stay with me
in time
be present
notice the dance in my heart
that hears only you
listen
my magnificent music
plays only for you
quietly
a tentative tune of trepidation
composed of egg shells
awaiting your return
for you to embrace me wholly
to feel our beat within.

Not your table

Sometimes you find
    there is no room at the table
    you approach
they move along
not to make room
but to make themselves
bigger
wider
obstructing the seat
eating quickly
devouring the space around them as if
nothing left
to share.

It's not your table.

Flowers from the Farm

It's about them
    not you
    the reason they don't make room
    don't squeeze yourself in
    you won't shrink to fit
    or accept leftovers
    crumbs of attention
    won't suffice
    don't stay
    politely say
    "Excuse me
    wrong table"
    move along
    find a space
    to sit comfortably
    find a feast
    filled with the flavours of friendship
    and if you ever hunger
    and need somewhere to dine
    remember
    I've saved you a seat at mine.

Sometimes

Sometimes
    I'm gone for days
    invisible for weeks

you text
    call
    knock on my door
    I don't reply
    my phone is on silent
    I'm not home.

Sometimes
    I am a superhero
    repairing her cape.

Sometimes I hide.

Burnout

Fire
    flames flicker
      close to centre
candles burning both ends
ash.

Pandemic mind

Wings clipped
    yet, not just mine
      only small steps allowed
must stay in line.
Don't travel they say
not safe to fly
they won't let you back in
less planes in the sky
told not to touch
warned not to breathe
all this containment
just feels too much
fear
suspicion
stupidity
surely we're better than this.
Please go out in the sunshine
and breathe in some bliss.

Clouds

Menacing dark clouds loom
    unveilingly around
    gloom
striving to surround
me in a diablerie of darkness
as black as the ocean of a starless night
I crawl
drowning
tumble
fumble
fall in a fluid flight
gasping in liquid pain
grip
slip into nothingness
weight in water
stumble in shadows of rain
beguiled by the blurry
bleary, teary, grey.

Treading water

I keep treading water
      despite depths
      dragging
me
down
tugging
lugging at my limbs
flooded by fears
submerged in tears
in sinistrous seas I struggle to swim
head just above water
gasp spit can't breathe
No.
I'll not let myself drown.

Rain

My eyes are full
 it's ok to cry
 rain
falls
down
when clouds get heavy
so
much
rain.

Safe in the dark

Under the covers
      no one can find me
      it's dark
safe
and the air I breathe
is just mine

glimmers of light sneak in
    remind me of the world
    just outside waiting

fear pulls me back
    tells me *it is warm in the dark*
    take the covers away
    the cold can get me
    can cut me rip
    tightness in my chest pulls at my throat

so I cannot breathe
unworthy.

I am never good enough
    stay here, fear calls me
    the blankets are heavy
    weight keeps me down in the softness of obscurity
    I can hold you here says fear
    no one can touch you
    nothing will hurt
    because nothing exists
    the empty space wraps you in blankets
    pulls you down
    burrow deep
    deep into the darkness.

It is safe in the dark.

Storm

Lost in a storm
      of confusion
         washed away
like driftwood
remnants
plastic bags
fishing line
tossed trash
tipped on the shore
bound by barnacles
waiting for the tide
to take me.

Grateful

I am grateful for the
    doors that have closed before me
    the unpleasant feelings
the hurt
the broken things
things fall apart - before falling back together
they protect me from the things not meant for me
things not meant to be.

Tired soles

I 've not walked in your shoes
      yet, I've noticed your step
      seems tired of late
soles worn thin
I give you my arm
to lean upon.
I shall try
to guide
you through.

Rise again

If I lose my spark
    I soon remember
       my soul is an ember
by my own breath's blow
it can gloriously glow
fuelling flickering flames
to make me rise again
like a mighty phoenix
with the whole damn fire.

GROWTH

Woman

Woman
 walked wearing the weight
 of the world's worries
on her shoulders
as if they were wings.

Sunday

Sunday
    always makes me think of
        someday
hours beyond now
we've not yet seen
a future hinted
an expanse of time glinted
in which what we seek
is still yet to occur.

Flowers from the Farm

Sunday
    sits somnolently suspended
    betwixt
    a week since ended
    and
    the beginning of the next
    not sure what to expect
    its continual contradiction
    of closure and commencement
    reminds us that
    before
    and
    after
    meet right now.

Sunday
    reminds me
    of the slipperiness of
    someday
    like greeting a fleeting thought
    before it leaves
    or turning an invitation
    into a meeting
    so as not to
    slide unseen.

Our future
    fast becomes the past
    unless we take it
    make it
    our now.

Our strength

Our strength
is in how we soften
as hard things
break too often.

On course

Energy flows
      where attention goes
      let gratefulness guide you
like a beacon of light
whilst the world's waves will overwhelm
hold love at the helm
steer thankful thoughts
to keep you on course
to your inner child be kind
please, my dear
take care of your mind.

Treasure within

Search within yourself
    for love
    for hope
for dreams
you'll discover them there
because that's where
true treasure has always been.

Inner child

Remember your worth
    it's time to play
       with your dear, sweet
inner child today
enjoy resplendent
rousing rides
the carousels
the swings and slides
lift up her hopes
her head held high
so the mirror's level
with her eyes
behold the most content reflection
of the one deserving your affection.

Little things

Strong women
　　treasure the little things
　　a hand held
a forehead kiss
the whisper of words
"you got this!"

My brother told me

Don't be tepid, nor scalding
    whilst your life is unfolding
    be white hot and passionate
la belle dames sans regrets
enjoy the dance
take a chance
embrace life's charms
with both brave arms
and savour its ever changing hues
that's what I've learnt from you.

Happiness is a choice

It is a blank page
    this day ahead
    as I wake
I can make of it what I wish
I can push aside
feelings of despair
replace them with bliss
I can decide
to draw in all corners
use all the colours
like the girl on the affirmations tape proclaims
I can look for positivity in my day
happiness is a choice
she tells me as I put on my socks
a choice I'm determined to make
though my mind is used to waking up
with worry, hurrying
for something
to be done

by my sharpened pencil
ticking lists
blurred by the slurs of smudged uncertainty
or pain to overcome
today I chose to start free
follow the flow of fluid lines
on white open spaces
I feel into the day
with crisp clear clean sheets
the paper on which I play
scribbled margins of ideas
erasing the fears
knowing I'm truly blessed
I must finish getting dressed
knowing that I'm loved
on earth and above
I like how she tells me
I can swim in pools of loveliness
I let her words wash my face in the mirror
as I decide not to hide behind
masks in my mind.
I allow myself to be clear
transparent
untainted by fear.
I can feel the colour of sunrise
touch my face
as I trace outlines of my dreams,
I choose happiness
I choose joy
I chase nothing but quiet contentment
knowing I have done what I wanted
composed what I chose
I will smile
I will glide

Melissa Domiati

I will feel full of love inside
the light
the colour
a gift from my mother
I will share it with others
I will warm the world with words
on this blank page of today
cool, white
exciting in its brightness
waiting to be written upon
the story I get to decide
as I step out into today.

Garden of friendship

Friends
      like flowers
      a mixed bunch
of colour
plant
water
dig
weed
they all begin as a seed
of familiarity
sunlight
helps flowers thrive
love keeps them alive.

Melissa Domiati

First flowers
    native
    suited to the soil
    rooted in the earth
    of childhood.

Exotic species
    from distant lands
    daffodils dance
    lilies lure us
    in a poignant perfumed trance
    their sweet scent
    lingering
    long since gone.

Fine formal flowers
    hot house roses
    upright stiff
    standing there
    no scent to share
    yet perfect somehow
    the facade of fun
    all they allow.

Wayward
    wild varieties of weed
    climbing
    invasive
    with thorns
    sometimes
    make us bleed.

. . .

Gentle comfort some
    like soft baby pink petals
    scattered on a bride
    they are a blessing
    nothing to hide.

Spring returns each year
    so do
    sublime sunflowers
    seeking the sun
    knowing they won't last forever
    they hold their happy heads high
    reminding us to be present
    letting their shadows fall behind.

My garden
    of friendship.

Wilting
    falling
    rooting
    rising
    blooming
    all love
    differing reasons and seasons.

Melissa Domiati

Nourish
    nurture
    feed
    dear friendships
    forever grateful
    together we grow
    tilting our faces to the sun.

You are the gardener of your friends.

My pool inside

It's so quiet in here
    so very quiet and still
    I can listen to the fill
of my own cup
with each
gentle
drop
I allow myself to stop
to believe
there is nothing I have to do
nothing I need to achieve
no one I need to see, or be
I can just breathe.

Melissa Domiati

It's so calm in here
    inside my own mind
    washed with the warmth
    of my own breath, I find
    I can rest
    within the
    rise
    and fall
    of my chest
    I can sit and feel
    all that is real.

It's so peaceful in here
    this tranquil pool inside
    wherein I give myself permission
    not to hide, but
    glide
    slide
    with the flow
    let my self-love grow
    I'm safe within myself
    I stay just as long as I need
    fortunate for me
    I never ever have to leave.

Here, in my clear
    space
    all thoughts are welcome
    embraced
    let go
    left to float for later
    in the distance

Flowers from the Farm

way across water
may rise ripples of regret
a slurry of worry
a heavy stagnant sludge of pain
dives in disdain
to dark depths down deep
rips and tides
try to pull me aside
I notice them
let them float past me
in here I will not
wallow in the shallows
of pity and despair
nor feel the bloodstained barnacles tear
I leave them to
drift
to
the
shore
for they can reside on the edge
washed up on the side
as I realise
I don't need them any more.

Later today
    if I should wish
    I may come out and play
    frolic
    flick
    kick
    splash
    dive
    from the high board

Melissa Domiati

down to the depths
dash
between duties and fun
swim up to the surface to see the sun
but for now
I surrender to my private pool
feeling how
buoyant in tranquillity
I glide
languidly lolling
rolling
I slide
fluid and free
I can just be
Quiet.
Calm.
Peaceful.
Me.

Sleep's sublime embrace

Seek solace in the silent space
    of sleep's sublime embrace
    slip softly in the sanctuary of slumber
you deserve its gentle grace.

Your pillow
    a billowy cloud
    in which you're allowed
    to let go, feel the slow
    surrender of worries and fears
    no need for them here
    let your breath exhale all stress
    and tranquillity hold you
    in its gentle caress.

Melissa Domiati

In this realm
    revel in release
    dance amidst constellations
    inner peace
    sway to the symphony of life
    hear your heartbeat music inside
    composed for your unique dance
    let it lead you in its tranquil trance
    let yourself go
    feel into the flow.

As shadows slip
    your soul resides
    in a quiet realm
    where peace and calm coincide
    while deep rest holds you
    in the folds
    sink into silken sheets of slumber
    take this time to allow
    your spirit to renew.

Let your dreams
    be a journey
    for you to feel free
    as your spirit takes flight
    follow moonbeams
    traversing the night
    stars whisper secrets
    in your mind
    unconfined.

A sacred space

Deep inside you
       within its own embrace
             sits
   a sacred space.

It waits
   patiently.

It has always been there
     like a favourite chair
     we often forget
     dash past in a hurry
     of flash and flurry
     yet
     it waits.

. . .

Melissa Domiati

With infinite patience
    calm and spacious
    your sacred space
    holds no trace
    of imperfections
    it's where reflections
    of pure light
    shine bright
    your place
    where nothing can reach you
    only the lessons
    that silence can teach you.

Within its exquisite solitude
    of strength and softness
    you are enough
    you may just sit inside
    this balm of calm
    quiet
    despite that which you
    may fight outside
    you are perfect just as you are
    stillness all around
    grounded
    by the earth's support
    surrounded
    by your own heart beat.

Flowers from the Farm

As you breathe
    tensions leave
    take in what you need to keep
    with inhales so deep
    of bravery and self love
    as you breathe
    tensions leave
    let go
    exhale
    what you don't need.

Trust
    that perfect moment
    always awaits you
    in your sacred space
    where you can discover
    your own gentle embrace
    of self love
    where you
    are free
    to simply be.

To be

To have a friend
        be a friend
                to be interesting
be interested
to be loved
love.

BLOOM

Bloom

We may feel we're breaking
    but branches bend
        flowers flourish in fine fragility
whilst watered
will not wilt

tilt your face
    towards the sun

let shadows fall
    behind you
        make room to bloom.

The first time

When your eyes held mine
      (that very first time)
        I fell for you
then you smiled
because you knew
at that moment
I knew
you loved me too.

Unlocked door

When I heard your voice
      that first time
      a door inside me opened
one that was locked
previously jolted
bolted shut
securely alarmed
protected from harm.

The cobwebs
    rust
    decay
    all fell away
    as the key turned
    bold, brass, solid
    click, it didn't stick
    turned so freely
    as you spoke in softness

Melissa Domiati

it opened wide
all the feelings inside
that I used to hide
could breathe fresh air
bathe in light
the delight
of feeling space
no trace
of hiding
colliding with the walls behind
once the door opened
I didn't want to leave
air
light
I could now hear myself breathe.

Our story

You fill my chapters with the words
    that comprise our story
        now I can sit up late at night
torch suspended under the bed covers
devouring all of the contents
guessing ahead
from that I've just read
to all of the pages
of our different ages
yet to occur
light shines on adventures with glee
happening to you
and to me
in my late night
reading and writing
I delight in
being inspired to compose
all the poems and prose
that comprise

Melissa Domiati

our lives through the dark of night
I hold tight
until sunrise
I know that if I sleep
my heart you keep
and I awaken
still
safe in our story of true love.

Morning

I awaken
    decadently drowsy
    with thoughts of you
your scent lingers
a breeze
of languorous longing
fills my senses
from when sunlight
clasped the earth
'til moonbeams kiss
tousled sheets
that take the shape of you
I slumber, somnolent
in love's perfect repose.

Love leapt in

Betwixt inhaling your essence
and exhaling all else
is when love leapt in.

The pleasure of your words

Seduce my mind
    with the pleasure
    of your words
my body will read them
and come
to its own conclusion.

He reads me

He reads me
    like a story in braille
        enamoured by my exposition
he feels me
unfolding my epic tale.

Tightrope

Enjoy the tantalising thrill
    arms outstretched
        feet tentatively placed
on the tightrope of life
hold your fabulous head high
then dance to the other side.

Love is a verb

Love is a verb
      the most wondrous word
      wherein we luxuriate
that infinite state
betwixt being, breathing
and unfailingly feeling
together we give
forever we live
entwined in actions
and reactions so grand
only our hearts understand.

Immortalised in ink

Love in ink
      indelible inscription
      of passion, honour and trust
ne'er in pencil or chalk dust
that maybe erased or may fade away.

Love not in blood either
    nor perspiration from fever
    as true love's anything but weak
    it sings songs the soul speaks
    of hearts and minds entwined.

Love immortalised in ink
    withstands the test of time.

Don't love in pencil

Love in pen
 permanent marker even
 smudges are ok
just don't love in pencil
it's too easy to erase.

Passion

An ember glows
    gentle breeze blows
    a flicker lifts with each breath
licks flicks
entices
the warm rises slowly
ashen scent of longing
falls down like snowflakes
rise and fall
growing with each breath
heat widens
red passion
prances, dances in the flames
crackle, cackles like a temptress
tantalising to behold
too dangerous to touch.

A giddy young girl

My heart skips
      flips
          dances and prances
with joy
when I meet the eyes of my boy.

The warmth in his smile
    makes my tummy twirl
    like a giddy young girl
    awaiting her first kiss.

Thinking of you

A simple fact
    that is so very true
        is that I am never ever
not thinking of you.

Retreat

Within me
is a distant land
fluent
in a language
only you can understand.

I love the way you love me

I love the way you hold my hand
    you listen, seek to understand
    my heart and
the melodious music of
it's beating parts.

I love the way you hold my eyes
    you adore me
    all the more, as we
    grow together
    know forever
    that we are worthy
    of our one true love.

Melissa Domiati

I love the way you hold my heart
    fragments of intense fragility
    once in parts
    now safe in your embrace

I love the way you hold
    the whole
    of my soul

I love the way
    you love me.

Whilst moonbeams trace

Drink me with thine eyes
    quench your thirst
    for wanting
as I move beneath you
satiate your hunger
as you slip your soul into mine
whilst moonbeams
trace
the shape
of us.

He loves me

H*e loves me.*

A thought she pulls up and over herself like a blanket
    warm
    safe
    as strong as silk
    soft
    like coming home
    to the crocheted cocoon of comfort
    Nanna May used to make.

He loves me.

As one

There is no you or I

our souls sigh
    in deep relief
    every night as we
    fall sleep
    in each others arms
    they rejoin
    complete
    as one.

Melissa Domiati

There is no you or I
    only us
    every night as our souls
    breathe
    wrapped in trust
    we rest
    together
    as one.

My world

Like being on holiday
      is a moment with you
      I dive into your eyes
they take me to places I've never been
or had the courage to dream
a spell of enchantment
weaved it's way into my heart
when you became my world.

I do

I do
    my love
    I ardently do
taste the freedom
embodied by our unconditional love
I do
see our enchanted eyes
as they embrace
feel our eager heart's truth
I do
hear our vow to cherish us
speak our pledge of trust in our union
I do
know the familiar feeling felt the first time we met
understand that our souls have known each other all their lives
I do
my love
I ardently do.
Like a fairytale come true - I marry you.

About the Author

Melissa Domiati (nee Tapper) is a Fremantle-born author, mother and educator with a passion for travel, poetry, life stories and empowering others to share their authentic voices. Her diverse professional life was rooted in commerce, when she realised she enjoyed words more than numbers, shifting her focus towards writing and international education.

Melissa is currently writing a collection of inspirational longevity stories, gleaned from people she is interviewing across the globe, together with a new poetry collection about cultivating calm.

She holds degrees in Commerce, Arts and Education and is a proud member of WA Poets Inc, Writing WA and The City Farm Writers Group in East Perth.

Her poetry has been included in numerous publications. *Flowers from the Farm* is her first solo collection of poetry. Melissa lives with her muse, her husband Salem, who is her biggest fan.

facebook.com/melissa.domiati.poetry
instagram.com/melissa.domiati.poetry
linkedin.com/in/melissa-domiati

www.ingramcontent.com/pod-product-compliance
Lightning Source LLC
Chambersburg PA
CBHW072001290426
44109CB00018B/2092